POETRY IS BALM

Poems and songs
for our
Grievous and Distracted Times

O.O. Bird

Image overleaf:

Hawaiʻi ʻŌʻō Bird (Moho nobilis);
tinted lithograph by John Gerrard Keulemans, c. 1895.

The ʻŌʻō Bird became extinct almost forty years ago:
what is believed to be the last existing recording
of the song of Moho braccatus, the Kauaʻi ʻŌʻō Bird,
was made by David Boynton in 1987.

POETRY IS BALM

Poems and songs
for our
Grievous and Distracted Times

by

O.O. Bird

CONTENTS

LOVE, LOVERS &
LE PLAISIR DE LA CHASSE:

SKETCHES & SENSATIONS:

THE COMING OF THE END:

EXEUNT:

PROLOGUE

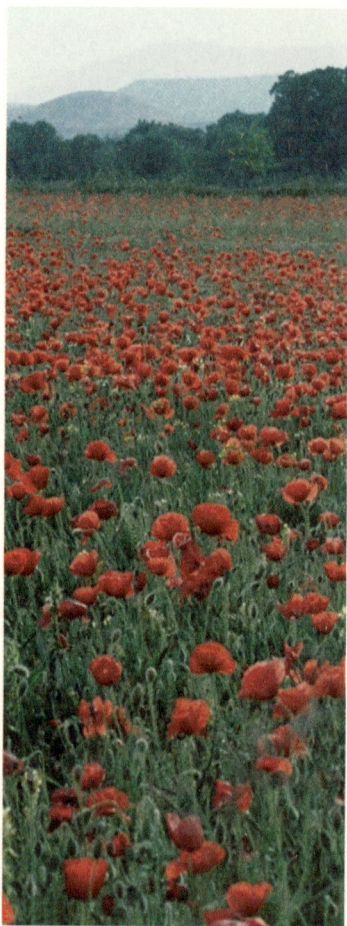

Poetry is Balm

Poetry is balm to the tormented valleys of the brain;
It comes as rainwater to the wells of the heart
And as shafts of sunlight among the dark hills
Of the liver. We feel it when we turn away.
We know it when it rises from inside
To palliate pain with its passing echo
Or to purge the secret tents of coiled-up evil.

On the battlefield, poetry is powerless to protect – poor soul!
But as night returns, she illuminates with song
The deep gorges wrought within us by fear,
By loss, by fruitless fighting and false hope.
With fresh flowers she renews the bloodied field,
Returning new life again to the valleys of the brain,
Slipping rainwater into the wells of the heart,
Sending long shafts of light far into the darkness
                    Of our livers.

Poetry is the soul – momentarily escaped
From the gravity of existence and thrust,
Like an astronaut, into the empyrean of words
To look down again, with longing, on our valleys
                    And lakes and oceanic depths.

LIFE,
SICKNESS,
&
DEATH

Mekong

As I behold you, my pulse slows:
The sliding surface softened and aged by sorrows,
The liquid that just flows, and flows and flows and flows –
Flowing for epochs before our birth, flowing as we die,
Flowing through warm processions of the nights in which we lie:
Flooding earthquake of measured motion,
Intent on nothing but the pull of distant ocean.
Great sustaining discharge of benignity;
Dark vein of massive movement; aqueduct of nature's dignity.

Million upon million raindrops, tears upon human tears,
Impenetrable, unchanging repository of years and years,
Drowning all loves, and questionings, and futile fears,
Flowing where brilliant calling-birds illuminate the leaves
In forest darknesses through which your glistening cleaves,
Cleansing and feeding life's fields in every moment,
Administering relief to the wearied elephant
That wallows like a shipwreck in the sunset sunlight,
Feeling that cool balm flow on, and on, and on, into night.

Calm River, be my lover, now! Lift me from my feet,
Take me twisting in the current's relentless sweep,
Content and unresisting, far into your water's deep.
You are the river of dreams, the magnet of life's forces,
Drawing strength from multitudes of seeping sources,
Gathering them into this confluence of existence,
Ceaselessly obedient to time's ceaseless insistence.

As I behold you, feel how my pulse slows.
Take me, dark waters, as the darkening evening glows,
Till I am one with the drowning quiet of your sound.
Silence the search for reasons that never can be found,
Wash to nothingness this place I was so proud to know.
Release me from the constant, fruitless push against the flow,
   And carry me lifeless down to the ocean's floor,
   Where nothing shall ever matter any more.

The meadow of life

Clear the field.
Prepare the field.
Sow the field.
Cultivate the field.
Reap the field,
And cherish the produce,
In a moment of
Quiet astonishment.

Then forget the field for ever,
Because you will go somewhere else.
Forget absolutely, and without regret.

Passing at a tangent

Sealed in the desert's envelope of silence,
Even the soundless grating of the clouds
Against the mountain ridge has stopped.
Shadows no longer steal against the light:
Utter, outer, unutterable calm, alone.

Dead trees hold their breath;
The earth dares not sweat
For fear of breaking the silence.
I, only, sitting motionless on a rock,
Think I hear perhaps the
Distant horn of mortality.

Anza Borego Desert

Transformation

As their brief life passes, the rose-flowers weep their petals.
It happens silently and with such simple sadness,
Fragmenting the perfumed majesty of their prime
Into scattered scraps, quite without order or meaning.
Their crumpled faces apologise mutely for their change.

How swiftly does that oversexed and silken perfection
Become something we can no longer even bear to behold.
The once sublime scent, and crafted orderliness is ruined:
We can only turn away our eyes, because it hurts so much,
With the hurt of dismay, of departure and defeat –
The hurt of all that enraptured beauty dissolving
Into disarray like an orchestra that has lost its way.

Perhaps too easy for the poet to liken the decomposing
Rose flowers to all that happens in our life: no prize for that...
And yet, as I look at them, transfixed by their brief story,
Longing to comprehend the meaning of their fallen tears
Across the floor, I know that I understand nothing – no more
Than any other person – about why we are born to such beauty,
Yet die in putrefaction.

Life from above

The sound of the city,
From the forty-fourth floor,
Is all but extinguished.

I look down on it,
As if on all the busyness
Of my own existence.

The sense is of unforeseen relief –
Like love for a person
Left long behind,

A place never to be entered any more.
The heart heals before this calming vision.
I shall not ask for it again;

But leave it, please,
As a marker in my life –
A sort of epitaph,

For when I step through
The sealed glass, and swoop
Into the hypnotised trees below.

Bangkok

21

Drowning

In the aquarium of life thoughts glide past
Like golden guppies or blue-finned inspirations,
Translucent, striped, in incandescent
Flits of rhythm – turning, pausing, like music
To the astonished ears of our minds.
Thoughts; single thoughts; shoals of thoughts,
Yearning to be followed down emerald glades
Of swaying vegetation to depths where
Untold galaxies of silver bubbles burst and rise.

But Nature knows otherwise, saying laughingly
To us: "Water is death to you by drowning!
Think! How will you feel as the water floods
The cavities of your throat and your eyes sink
And sink, and your thoughts like golden guppies,
Mute, uncaring, pull you, pull you over the brink?"

24

Them

(dedicated to all those who suffer migraines)

See this hammer of solid sterling silver,
Ice-cold to the touch, sleek to the eye?
Take it, long prepared, from the darkness
    Of the freezer.

Take aim carefully, and do not flinch.
Here's the place – here, here... Here it sits,
The toad that feeds on flesh and sleep
    And sanity.

This corner, just behind the eye – take aim
And bludgeon it... *Again*. Again… again,
Till the poison has all leaked out from within
    The fractured skull.

If, with that release, life must ebb too, I rejoice
To feel it ooze from me as the price of freedom.
Just promise me, Death, that beyond that end
    They, *they* will be no more.

A Lifetime's Work

O fields of failure spread before me,
And unrequited calls from far below:
O rolling hills of ripe regret
Awaiting the reaper long-since dead.

How poignant from this point of vantage,
How silent is your timeless reproach!
The songs you sent were magic,
But their music stolen by the wind.

Hard harvest of my soul's torment,
Bitten by winter in the flower of promise,
What more hurt can you give me, now
Your season is past and my soul has dried?

As I look, I bleed – not blood,
But iced dismay. O fields of failure!
What chill upon the soul of fantasy
Blasts these pastures of the past!

Words will not come, nor prayers,
Nor protestations – just numbness
Without hope, chokes this sight of
Field upon fresh field of failure.

Pian del Vantaggio

Daffodil time

Let me die in fullest daffodil-time,
When all is yellow and scented fresh,
When the air is crisp and laden
With expectation of a million flowers,
Leaves and grasses, and yet more
Daffodils and jonquils, yellow and white,
Incarnate for a lingering moment.

Yes: I shall try to die in fullest daffodil time,
With birds and madness in the air,
Song and flight and rain and light –
Not black serge and stuttering sadness.
Let my body not be seen for all the daffodils
There will be! Their bright, light texture,
Scented with hope, shall long outlast the bones
Of my brief sojourn in their home.

Swallow song

In the air, a thousand feet above the sea,
These swallows – do they enjoy their acrobatics?
Finessing currents far above the cliffs,
And careening along the roofs of village streets,
Descending to our world just to drink, or replicate
Their quintessential being in calm,
Enamel firmaments, hidden from sight and harm.

Sentinels of spring and sempiternal symbols
Of companionship, journeyers and free spirits of the aether:
Next time around, I want to enter your enamel universe,
To stir within the sightless cosmos of an egg,
And then break out from the warmth and start to fly,
Almost invisible, and untouchable by anything but death –
In the air, a thousand feet above the sea.

PEOPLE
&
PLACES

Adam

Adam was a strange boy,
Profoundly affected -
Wounded, I would say -
By the events of his life.

Privileged by his birth,
Yet with a distant father
And a mother he never knew,
He grew much in solitude.

Working, sometimes walking,
Beneath the trees or in the rain,
His body was shaped by thought,
By movement, and by labour.

His thinking was good-natured,
And nature, in turn, was good
To him – trying to make up
For all that had gone wrong
            In Eden.

Yet often when he heard a bird
Sing out in the cadenced silence,
Its chanting melody
Would shock and infuse

His being with such spaciousness
And longing, that he wanted only
To be naked once again with nature,
In his hallowed oak-brown skin.

The memories were bitter-sweet;
And the delving of the song
Transported him to realms far
From his, far from happy, self.

He made sure that she – his partner –
Was distant at those moments,
So that his nakedness
Might not be misunderstood.

Samothrace

The morning is perfect, and full of the sound of birds;
But my heart is a hollow waterfall
Hidden from sight in mountain forest fastnesses,
Forging, falling, always falling
Through spaces full of birdsong,
Deaf to death and every sound
Save, when in the lap of fallen boulders,
It pens into a pool and pauses for a moment –
Still enough to reflect the perfect dawn –
Before seeking once again new falls, new ways to fall,
On and on, through forest fastnesses
And spaces without birdsong, falling beneath
The roots of trees where nothing can be heard
But the constant falling, the sacred, endless falling
Beyond which there is nothing but the loss,
The loss of life and of the sound of birds
And yet more forest fastnesses for falling.

In an earlier life I was a vase,
But now I am become a waterfall,
A waterfall I cannot stop from falling,
Or from seeking what it only ever sought
In the lifeless anonymity of the open sea.

To an unknown traveller
on a delayed flight
at Bari Airport

Thank you for being.
Thank you for making this purgatory a joyful journey
Simply by existing with your unassuming beauty,
Transforming all that was just noise and irritation
Into a surge of revelation.

I observed every detail of how you are,
Of how you dress, with what naturalness of movement,
Feeling tides of gratefulness push over me
Just for having shared with you the same transience
Of time, and space, and presence.

How strange it is to want to shower with blessings,
A person I never knew nor will ever see again,
To feel this out-bursting of goodwill
In wishing that ugliness and harming strife,
Might never ever come near you in your unknown life.

Or will that unique being of yours,
Cross my path again in quite another form,
Unexpectedly and in quite another time?
And will I know you to be the same, and sense
Again that same humble, yet sublime, essence?

Hadrian's visit

The Emperor Hadrian came.

Stepping through the kitchen door, he entered – or else was ushered in
By some invisible agent – and stood before me, bemused, a little reticent,
Clearly unsure of what was going on; shy, as if, for the first time,
He, the Emperor, was quite nonplussed by his surroundings.

He was much smaller than I imagined, swarthy, quite solemn.
"A coffee?" I wondered, but, no, that would not be appropriate.
In the end, just a glass of crystalline water. After a while,
He spoke hesitantly, but I could not understand a word.
And if I spoke, he looked horrified at first, and then confused.

He stayed four days, clearly not at ease, except when he took a bath:
That, at least, was comprehensible to him.
He did not wish to be disturbed, but I think he slept very little.
It was strange to see one as great as he, so manifestly troubled.
Then on the fifth morning he was gone, nowhere to be seen.

I asked my neighbours, and all around the village,
But nobody had seen anything. It was hard to explain, as well.
On the fifth day, it seems, he just rose from the living world
And went to heaven for all I know, or back to the land of the dead,
And simply left behind, with me, an unmade bed.

He came and went, all unannounced. It was some strange crease
In time that brought him here – far from Etna's sunrise, far
From tragic Egypt, and from the willowed streams of Gaul; far from
That deep shaded garden in Tibur, where he was perfectly Emperor,
Among fireflies and nightingales, who knew not who he was.

I wanted afterwards to say to him: "Hadrian, I know:
So rich, so unforgettable, the music of this world –
But cling to it no more, relieve the spasm of your memory,
Pass on to new worlds, unimaginable and far.
Leave behind the ashes of Antinous, and of all your loves.

Yet I could not find the language, nor the words to say it.
How could I change the nature of his fate? For he was gone.

Kythera burnt, August 2017

(The island of Kythera was sacred to Aphrodite in Antiquity.
In August 2017, almost 20% of the island's green cover
was burnt by wild-fires)

Aphrodite appeared to me, all dressed in black.
"You did not expect me to come like this, did you?
You did not think I would allow my home to suffer
The destruction of his voracious hurricane of heat?
I did it, because he is my husband, because we, too,
Were lovers once, because he had become jealous,
Too jealous, of the much-praised beauty of my home.

And so I let him destroy it, opening the doors
Of his forge, goading out his beast with iron tongs
Till it flooded through the plains and gorges
In a senseless fury, eating everything in its path.
Only this could quench his jealousy for a while.
So do not complain: you brought it on yourself,
By not attending to my needs as much as to your own."

It's true, I expected nothing of this – nor her charcoal lips
So close to mine, nor the dead and cavernous voice.
It was the utter contrary of love; the undoing of all
That soft green life of living trees and grass.
I tried and tried to awaken from this smoking dream,
But to no avail. She held me in so hard an embrace.
And grim Hephaistos looked on with satisfaction.

At Phanai

Alone that day along the shore I found no precious stone,
No bright shell to charm its way into my pocket,
No rare flower, no bird – just unconfined tranquillity.

A herd of goats, at first uncertain, paused and would not pass
Until I rose from my seat and walked away from them.
At first they followed, curious … then left in search of food.

The sun descending; the breeze rising; the platinum light of January –
No desire, just the gnawing yearn for Antiquity.

Huntington Gardens, LA

Such peace at the centre
In this sacred patch – the quadrant
At the heart of a mandala, where nothing stirs
Yet everything is intently alive.

Uncreated blue, the mountains and the sky,
And all around the city slowly
Formiculates, for it is Sunday,
And calm telepathises from soul to soul.

Somewhere behind me breaks the song of a bird
Which for too long I have not heard,
Saying nothing, yet crying clearly out
From oceans long unvisited within.

For a moment there is everything.
The pursuit of things is far away.
Time runs no more, but falls
In welcome showers of green.

How simple, how complete the solution seems –
How simple, letter by letter, the utterance
Of the soul – the song of the bird,
For ever half-heeded, for ever half-heard.

For a moment it lingers, loth to leave,
Then falls silent. And in that silence,
There is no city any more, but just the
Firmament of stars as it was in childhood.

LOVE,
LOVERS
&
le Plaisir de la Chasse

The Harbour

In the quiet harbour of my arms
No harm shall come to you, my love;
Be still and drink in peace
The circle of infinity they enfold.
Tied to the moorings of my heart,
No earthly trouble can disturb
The limpid depths of your repose
Or undo the intertwinings
Of our lives of sea and earth.

I am your harbour wall, rooted
In the seabed's rock. It is not
Storms I fear, nor winds, nor flying spray,
But that morning of unforeseen stillness,
Full of fragrant promise,
When the silent sun bleeds veins
Of bright copper light across the ocean's skin,
And, in its thrall, you set out once again
For home in the radiant East.

Come, love, leave your soul behind
In this green world – in these hidden places
Where swans dabble with their young
Among the reeds and swaying branches;
Let something of you stay behind to keep
The perfume of your presence hanging still
Like jasmine on summer nights in those gardens
Where we met and walked and kissed and loved
Like blessed fools without a future or a past.

Sonnet, in 17th Century style

(1982)

When in the brilliant company of friends,
I to thy face cast back my longing thought,
Then would I go to the planet's ends
To seek thee out – so chargèd is my heart.
For, in the miracle of thy sweetness,
I read the pleasure of eternity
And in thy eyes am lost in quietness
Amidst the concourse of activity.
The seasons, nights and distances are as naught
To me; and though I would at once take leave
And come, thou knowest not how I am caught
In thy enchantment yet. Unseen I grieve
  That for to have thy love, I must cross fears
  Greater by far than distances and years.

Summer nights in Rome, on the Tarpean Rock

On summer nights in Rome,
When soft was the stone in the warmth of its shadow,
And meadow paths of cobble-stones glistened to the moon,
Amid towering ruins like trees, and low-lit portals crouched about by cars,
Then would I dress myself in rough simplicity,
And – drawing breath across the emptied square –
Make my way towards the fountain once again,
Happy in pursuit, hot heart in mouth, and shod with a joyous fear.

Through those deep-delved streets,
I went each night to quench my thirst at that same source –
To hear its gentle sound unchanged, and watch its reflections shimmer out
Forms imagined, real, and soft of touch, to fill the basin of desire with dreams.
In the swinging shadows of the trees,
Silent, save for the close breath of footfall,
They passed and paused and glimpsed
And circled in the ceaseless dance of courtship.

In those far off days I was always close
To the fountain – its waters flowed and flowed, and never dried:
Hours into the warm night, the arching pines would watch our dance below,
And birds would sleep with open eyes, as calm as spirits from a distant age.
Ignorant of what this strange
Fusing of so many centuries might mean,
We drank the tragic thrill of kissing
On rocks where slaves and traitors had once been tossed to oblivion.

My friends, the stars

I stepped out of the gateway into the dark,
And the thousand upon thousand of stars,
     Were suddenly my friends.
The warm night air was the embrace I had longed for,
And the profiled shadow of the hills beyond was like a body,
     Asking in stillness to be explored.

In my youth I had followed those invisible paths,
Seeking out the darkest recess where twilit chance
     Might momentarily be my friend.
That was the annihilating embrace I longed for then;
But now the stars are my true companions, on our silent,
     Solitary dance into the dawn.

Keramoto.

Chan

Chan. Chan. I came to your call.
Along the backward river-bed of time, I came again
For you – for the memory of you, of you and me
Fused in those searing days, poised at the horizon of time
        Of thirty years ago.

Chan. You pull me East again.
Always Eastwards, back to that damp chasm of warmth
Where my desire was born, and your face was formed,
And a myriad others also, dear to me for they lead me
        Back, back again to you.

Chan, you wake in me fires I cannot hold,
Stirrings I cannot contain, things that do not belong
In this world, but somewhere altogether other –
Beyond that chasm of warmth without walls where there was just
        You and me and nobody else.

Chan, Chan… while you slept, I watched,
Paused and marvelled at the effortless sculpture
Of your being, at the bloom and colour that the filtered
Morning light revealed of you, your gentle falling breath,
        And the soft touch of your motionless feet.

You were away; but I never left my vigil by your side.
How often would it be, in intervening years,
That your image would come to me in company,
Through warmth or aching solitude, to administer that perfume
        From the other world where you
           Alone lay next to me.

Today my head is full of Puerto Rico

Today my head is full of Puerto Rico –
The crazy vegetation, its laughing music,
And the sunlight in its twenty-year old boys.

By that engulfing sea, in that twilight warmth,
I lost my heart, I lost my head
Again and again, just as I lost it
On the Tarpaean Rock and on the walls
Of Rhodes, at Kochin, Zamalek,
Zamboanga and in a thousand other warm
And silent and somehowever secretive places,
Where, speechless, yet with that same conspiring
Vegetation and perhaps some distant laughing music,
I learned to find the unmistakeable inner sunlight
Of those aching twenty-year old bodies.

All that is past. It is strange
How I have simply aged and they –
By what magic art? – have stayed the same,
Always twenty, perhaps nineteen even,
But with that self-same sunlight
Burning beneath the same untried skin,
Like a perfect fig, like an earthquake
Deep below the ground, far from sight.

O distant island in the sea,
How soon you set me free!

Brief Encounter
with tropical fruit

What squalid favella brought forth this exquisite creature?
What rotten food fleshed out the soft, unblemished
Contours of this body, dark as lamp-lit nightfall?
What sights nourished these perfected limbs,
And the flow of every concavity, and the thick black hair,
And that divine and overarching perfume?

The favella's rich manure brings forth – yes – such wondrous fruit.
Through a poverty doused with sunlight and cleansing rain,
Ripening with a warm and easy beauty. I feel the firm texture of it
Against my tongue, and its life-giving juice fills my mouth.

I was black once

Tall black man in the candy-stripe shirt,
How I love the way you flirt.
What vistas does your smile awaken…!
O, tell me not your heart is taken.

Tell me not that shy embrace
Is only for another's face.
How far from perfect, to have to share
The secret of such playful fare!

The play, of course, is not for me.
But… what if the strings of fate were broken free,
And I could know, for one eternal night,
That warmth your skin keeps hidden from the light?

Then, how easy would I fly back through the ages,
Through the landscapes, through the thousand pages
Of the story of my soul, like a well-aimed dart,
To all those previous moments in which I knew your heart.

Tall black man, with your smile so free,
You are the mirror in which I see
Myself afresh, just as I was in many lives before –
A being with that joyful darkness at its core.

Then came Hector

Then, after a long succession of indifferent fighters –
Brave, but inconsequential, untutored, and without true art –
Then, at last, came Hector, prince of warriors,
Whose eyes spoke ardour and his demeanour war,
But nobler war, gentler, truer, artful, irresistible war;
Hector, who could disarm even with an innocent smile,
Who knew, from the instinct of his princely birth, the art of combat,
Exactly how to parry and play and lead on his prey
Through labyrinths of shining strokes, retorts and thrusts,
Onwards, unstinting, even to the point of utter exhaustion,
Before letting that bright sword free to perform its magic –
That sword, a gift of the gods, so hard for mortals to resist!

But, O Hector, what avails your great art
And all your rare and noble gentility,
When, at the end, your royal blood shall be spilled
In gasping agony, like any common wretch,
And flow unstopped there where we lie together
Locked in that final, fatal embrace?

Lycian Morning

In the uncertain morning light,
As the ship pushed deeper, deeper
Into that warm fissure of the Lycian coast,
And all those on deck held their breath at
The fresh-released beauty that opened all around,
I heard the anchor drop,
And knew it was the anchor of my life –

Never before so quick, so sure
To plumb the depths I prayed I'd never
See again. Confounded beauty!
Sent to torment my uncertain soul
For the faltering failure of its motion,
Frozen and condemned to swallow salt and iron
In one hurtful blow against the bedrock floor.

Love, we lay together only in our fantasy,
In that beautiful morning never to be repeated:
I have you only in the vagueness of memory,
Of another age, another life, another body
Where the soft smell of warmth was everything...
The recollection is no more than a sinking
To that sea-bed whence little is ever reclaimed.

Your body is the earth on which I lie

(A Song of Love)

Your body is the earth on which I lie –
Bound to its chestnut colour below the sky;
Soft as the soil that takes my weight,
It is the ground beneath my fleeting fate.

Circling through nocturnal space
Held fast in your unseeing embrace...
How strange that all this makes me feel
A solitude that will never heal.

Release these arms, release this grip,
Release our embrace, lip to lip,
And, as a climber from a mountain face,
Let me slip and fall and stall through space.

Solitary we were born, and solitary we shall die.
Solitary in the sick-bed where we lie,
We know this deep within the marrow of the bone:
Seeking love, we learn to be alone.

SKETCHES
&
SENSATIONS

Betrayal

Yes, gratefully, I slept in his bed.
Like courteous Duncan, who relished
The sweet and swallow-filled air
With gratitude, praising its beauty
With the stilted demeanour of royalty –
I, too, unthinking, slept as his guest.

My mind raced awhile with scenes of carnage;
The sounds of distant revelry below
Came for long enough to my ears.
But as the moon sank, I surrendered
To a deep, deserved repose
The like of which I had never felt before.

Doggerel on Godderel

A dog needs no god,
Alpha-dog is its god.
We too need alpha-dog,
So we create God.

Reassuring, but a waste of time,
Because alpha-dog is just a dog,
Like any other dog, not a God.

Alpha-dog needs a pack,
Just as God needs one, too.
So we, in turn, create our pack,
With extra-ordinary religious knack.

Reassuring, but a source of strife,
Ruin to any hope of harmony in life.
When, I wonder, will we learn?
Dog needs no god, and nor do we.

Reading a poem

I read Gray's *Elegy* in the stillness of this morning.
Absorbed in its cadences, I slipped back into sleep again
And dreamed vividly of blue irises in clear running water
Flowing through the rock-scape of my hand,
In channels between fingers and knuckles of eroded stone.

Strange, because there are no irises, nor blue, nor water
In the poem – nothing that they share in that.
Yet what I felt was something else, an unheard music
That yoked them together in far deeper kinship,
Sunk from sight beneath the genial current of the soul.

At an onsen in Nara

Japan. One-thirty am. Torrential rain outside.
Went downstairs, half-asleep,
And slid into the hot water – my body
Flooding with unstoppable comfort.

My legs and feet stretched in front of me,
Grateful, healthy, relaxed beneath the surface.
Then a voice, quite suddenly, said to me,
Addressing me by my name:

"Very soon, you are going to die:
Prepare yourself now for the long journey."
I questioned if this voice was real.
Again: "Make yourself ready for the journey."

I looked at my legs and felt the pain of gratefulness
For the friendship of so many years together:
And then I thought of the journey ahead, and smiled,
As a surge of anticipation suffused my soul.

Lavender Dove in the Frangipan Tree

Lavender dove in the frangipan tree,
Poised between firmament and tropical sea,
You rest among branches of coral in the air
And naked flowers, like scented stars, everywhere.

You look. You tilt your head. And look again,
At peace, at ease, with undisturbed attention –
Mistress of tranquillity amid the turbulence all around
Of swirling tides and indistinguishable sound.

I pray for Nothingness, and her sister, Release,
In spontaneous words of healing peace.
Unobserved, unfelt, the glittering casket slips from me –
Words, images, promises, thoughts and aspirations
      For ever at the bottom of a warm, clear sea.

Thailand

THE COMING
OF THE END

Before the ruination comes

Before the ruination comes,
There is the moment of perfect beauty,
A timeless pause of visionary stillness.
The sky, the sea, the distant mountains,
Will all be stilled in contemplation,
And look upon the silence that separates them
              With embodied calm.

Nature gives so much to us: we often cannot hold it.
It is a fullness too great to comprehend,
Over-filling the fractured cup we tend.
It awakens that pain which music often brings,
Hurting where the joy of recognition leaves us in dismay,
Speaking for us the words that were in our heart,
              But which we could not say.

As time slows and halts, as at a junction,
There will open up a moment such as this –
Where the distant antiphon of birdsong,
Measures the depth across the silent gorge,
And even the motionless odour
Exhaled from the grass, appears to understand,
              Accepting what will come.

Before the ruination comes, we will feel no boundary
Between the gorge without, and the space
Within our hearts – the one becomes the other.
Such calm is a gift to remind us of what will be destroyed,
For everything will change, after the long waiting
For the ruination; and this perfect beauty will be no more
              Than a snatch of passing song.

When the oceans of the world have drained away

When the oceans of the world have drained away,
And the long sound of their draining has ended
In an unexpected silence;
And when the hot winds have dried to dust
The immensities the seas once occupied,
And they too have dropped to silence
Because there is nothing more to dry;
Then those who remain – if any remain –
Will hear eerie strings of sound descend,
As of Sirens' songs, but yet more strange –
Luminous strings, till now unheard,
Filling the furrowed firmament above.
And those who can grasp them will at last
Be lifted lightly to another world, far away,
And glimpse fleetingly below the Prince of Darkness,
Solitary on his rotting bark, victorious on this planet
That so exercised his love of emptiness.

EXEUNT

These Poems

Dear God! thank you for these poems…
These little shreds of soul,
Grated from the fragrant, blemished rinds of sensation.
I know not what I would do in life without them.
I hold them close to me – as precious as any children.

Yet, whose are they? Yours? Mine? Someone else's?
Some reader's, out in Africa, who found them on a 'plane?
If all and everything of me is erased in this world,
Will I one time meet them again in another life,
Hiding in a corner, or flying in, unannounced
Through a window of light,
And speaking in a different tongue?

First published in 2025
by
Genius Loci Publications,
<geniusloci.publications@gmail.com>
on behalf of
The Anargha Poetry Circle.

ISBN 978-1-0369-1630-5

Book Design by David Gillingwater,
Herring Bone Design Ltd.,
Suffolk.

Printed in the United Kingdom,
By Short Run Press Ltd.,
Exeter, Devon.